A Late Spring, and After

Also by Robert B. Shaw

Poetry
Aromatics (2011)
Solving for X (2002)
Below the Surface (1999)
The Post Office Murals Restored (1994)
The Wonder of Seeing Double (1988)
Comforting the Wilderness (1977)

Criticism
Blank Verse: A Guide to its History and Use (2007)
The Call of God: The Theme of Vocation in the Poetry of Donne and Herbert (1981)

As Editor
Henry Vaughan: Selected Poems (1976)
American Poetry since 1960: Some Critical Perspectives (1973)

A Late Spring, And After

Poems

Robert B. Shaw

PINYON PUBLISHING
Montrose, Colorado

Copyright © 2016 by Robert B. Shaw

All rights reserved. Except as permitted under the U.S. Copyright Act of 1976, no part of this publication may be reproduced, distributed, or transmitted in any form or by any means, or stored in a database or retrieval system, without the prior written permission of the publisher, except for brief quotations in articles, books, and reviews.

Cover Art:
The Upper Reaches of the Tama Water Supply Flowing through the Koganei Embankment from *A Mirror of Famous Rivers in the Eastern Capital*

Woodblock print by Utagawa Hiroshige (1797-1858)

Copyright © 2016 by Victoria and Albert Museum, London

Photograph of Robert B. Shaw by Hilary A. Shaw

Design by Susan Elliott

First Edition: August 2016

Pinyon Publishing
23847 V66 Trail, Montrose, CO 81403
www.pinyon-publishing.com

Library of Congress Control Number: 2016945820
ISBN: 978-1-936671-38-0

Acknowledgments

Some of these poems have appeared in the following publications:

Alabama Literary Review: "Dinosaur Tracks," "'Pity the Monsters!'," "On the Death of Wilmer Mills"

Hopkins Review: "Craquelure," "Handiwork"

Pinyon Review: "Selection," "Before My Eyes," "Her Mother's Seashell," "September Toadstools," "A Confirmation," "Your Hand," "Through a Glass, Darkly," "Eight Months Later," "My First Atlas," "Cézanne: 'The House with the Cracked Walls'," "Voice Mail"

Southwest Review: "News Item"

Umbrella: "An Arrangement of Dried Flowers"

Yale Review: "Sensitive Plant," "The Tally," "The Loss of the Joy of Cooking," "Afterthought"

"Three Riddles from the Exeter Book" appeared in *The Word Exchange: Anglo-Saxon Poems in Translation*, ed. Greg Delanty and Michael Matto (New York: W. W. Norton, 2011).

For Hilary

At first I thought to say "in memory,"
but the words feel inert for what I feel.
Even at rest you go the rounds with me.
You are the steadfast axle, I the wheel.

Contents

I: VESSEL

My First Atlas   3
Craquelure   5
Selection   7
Handiwork   8
Wear   10
A Beacon   12
The Custody of the Eyes   13
The Wish Bone   15
Cézanne: "The House with the Cracked Walls"   16
Vessel   18

II: NOW WE NOTICE

Before My Eyes   23
Sun Shower   25
Dinosaur Tracks   26
Belligerents   27
"Pity the Monsters!"   29
The House of the Tragic Poet   31
Lachrymatory   33
On the Death of Wilmer Mills   35

A Confirmation   36
September Toadstools   37
Winter Stars   38
Hanging On   39
An Arrangement of Dried Flowers   40
Now We Notice   42

III: A LATE SPRING, AND AFTER

The Tally   45
What Happened   47
A Late Spring   51
The Loss of the Joy of Cooking   52
Voice Mail   54
Your Hand   55
Clockwork Sonnet   56
The Sun Room Plants   57
Fluid Ounces   58
Through a Glass, Darkly   59
Afterthought   60
Eight Months Later   61
Envoy   63

IV: FERRYING

By the Pond   67
Three Riddles from the Exeter Book   69
Paths Crossing   72
News Item   73
Shared Habitat   75
Lapcat   77
Sensitive Plant   79
New Year's Wish   80
Her Mother's Seashell   81
An Early Skirmish   83
Transformation Scene   84
Ferrying   85
Winter Sunset   87

Notes   90

I

Vessel

MY FIRST ATLAS

was not a book but a lamp,
a night light with attitude,
centered on the hall table
in the first house I lived in.
There, in my grandparents' manse,
I stood eye-level with this
half-squatting roustabout, this
hood who looked a good deal like
a hood ornament in style.
Musclebound, with a finish
mimicking bronze, he no doubt
was pot metal through and through.

None of this mattered as much
as what the small weightlifter
was charged to keep supported
with straining arms and shoulders:
a glass globe, so much bigger
than any part of his bulk.
Only alight at night time
or on a dark afternoon,
its will-o'-the-wispish glow
wasn't one you could read by:
it kept you from stubbing your toe.
The glass had little color
until the fifteen-watt bulb
inside it flickered to life:
then it appeared as green as
a honeydew melon's flesh.
Strange molded patterns on it
probably mapped the heavens

legend asserts he upholds,
and must, to the end of time.

Next door to this, on Sundays
in his church my grandfather
held up Heaven as a thing
that sensible people should
remember to aspire to.
At night, when the other lights
were out, the glow from the hall
was just enough to lead one
to the foot of the first flight
of stairs that climbed and twisted
up into quiet darkness.

Where could the eight-inch giant
have gone to? Perhaps the glass
got broken, or someone thought
he wasn't worth rewiring.
Now in the back of my mind
he turns out to be more than
just one kind of an atlas.
He helps me find a route back.
His green light tells me to go
past him again into rooms
where all the past lies asleep.

CRAQUELURE

The ancestors were more relaxed than some
when sitting for their portraits, given that
the painter was their son, presumably
performing gratis. In their Sunday best,
they peer shrewdly from their his-and-hers
twin ovals now exactly as they've done
for something like a century-and-a-half.
His formal white cravat, the filmy bands
depending from her lace cap set off healthy
complexions, features glowing with composure,
hair brushed to a sheen; in short, the earmarks
of prosperous middle age. A bead of white
glimmering from each pupil works to bring
their eyes to life. When I first pondered them,
flanking my grandparents' fireplace,
they did not seem approachable by children—
too venerable, even though their brows
were mostly free of wrinkles. Now I find
I've not only approached them but outpaced them,
drawn past their age that day they gave their son
his chance to practice on familiar subjects.

Immunity to mutability
confers on anyone a great advantage,
and for years I credited them with it.
Their sameness cast a spell of reassurance
on any of the parlors they were hung in.
Children of the latest generation
have had their turn at being sobered by them,
subdued to order by their steady gaze.
Lately, though, by sidling close enough

to give them a more skeptical inspection,
I've seen what doesn't show up from a distance:
clinging to each unworried face a wealth
of radiating fissures forming nets
of lines as delicate as hairs that once
were snugged together on the artist's brush-tip,
the one he favored for his finest strokes
to show posterity his parents' eyebrows.
Imagine filaments as fine as those,
spreading a weft, on each a weightless veil,
as if to compensate, year after year,
for all the wrinkles that would never show
in either likeness anchored to its canvas.
An aging in the surface of the paint
or in the once-protective coat of varnish
belies their images' arrested aging.

By now I'm used to this, but at the moment
it first came home to me, I thought of times
I'd made my way with care across a sheet
of pond ice till the cracks began to fan
out from my feet, warning me to back off.
Thank you, great, great Grandmother and Grandfather,
for offering a modicum of caution
along with your unruffled optimism.
No doubt you found this out before I did:
sooner or later, cracks are bound to come,
however safe our customary frames
prompt us to feel; the ice cannot be trusted
beyond a point we only recognize
on reaching it. Here, there's no turning back.

SELECTION

Matter-of-factly and midwesternly,
but with a faint shade of awe or relish,
"Struck by lightning," folks out at the farm
always got around to specifying
at times when their ill-fated former neighbor
came up in conversation. Listening,
I heard it as a single ominous word
rubbed smooth by an Ohio slur
(struckbuhlightnin). I was one of those
children with big ears, and hearing this
gave me a tingle, thinking of the reach
of savage talons ripping the night sky
we blinked at sometimes, out there in the summers.
The bone-white fire of heaven paid its visits,
so we were told, uncannily at random:
Oh, it could happen to anyone at all,
they said, caught out there under the wrong cloud.
But no, it happened to just this one they knew
(I felt like shouting, didn't even whisper),
to one they used to wave at in the field,
someone they traded tools with. That was what
struck me, not the jeopardy that reigned
aloof in cloudy generality
(by then I knew that everybody had
an expiration date); not that, but this
unshunnable, particular pinpointing
with all its mix of chance and choice for someone—
his instant, never dreamt-of claim to fame.

HANDIWORK

Against the back wall of our garage
my grandfather built a long workbench
on which whatever else we wanted
to have built for us would assume form
beneath hands that knew the ways of wood—
which meant his, plainly. My left-handed
father had no knack for carpentry,
no liking, either, but was more than
willing if the old man had a mind
to put tools smartly through their paces.
Coffee tables, cupboard shelves and doors,
bookcases, trellises and easels,
more and less structural joinery
filled his hours when he visited.
He let me heft with my untutored
hands the implements that in his hands
were like deft bodily extensions.
The handles I liked most to handle
looked like lemon jelly petrified.
Even now I have a mental grasp
of gear going about its business
capably or hung ready to hand
on hooks, or stowed on shelves: the sharp ones
he warned me about (planes, chisels, saws),
the three hammers (tack, claw, and ball-peen);
screwdrivers and wrenches in their ranked
sizes, and the spirit level with
its bubble that would never tell a lie.
Most of all I liked (I wonder why)
the pencil that he marked lumber with.

Flat, unfaceted, so it would not
roll out of sight or onto the floor,
its wooden shaft glowed tomato red.
He scored a dark line to guide his saw;
on each graphite track the saw bit down.
Sawdust from his cuts gleamed in sun-pools,
spilling down like sand in an hourglass.
Unhurried, he paid no heed to time,
had for company his tuneless hum.

If I had that pencil in my hand,
could I draw with it a straight, true line
from where I am back to where we were?
Dream on: too much has been put away
beyond reach of recollecting hands.
Just so, he made things neat, still humming,
when a day's work was done.

                                        When he died
the tools were orphaned, shunted into
an uneasy afterlife of scant
use and little skill. My parents moved;
the workbench, being built-in, stayed put
in the vacant, swept garage, its bulk
filling up the far end, standing bare
like a deconsecrated altar.

WEAR

Day after day after day,
when he sat down or stood up,
my father grabbed the arm-ends
of the captain's chair reserved
for him at the table's head.
His daily use over time
darkened the arms' finish,
leaving, as even a clean
hand will, anointings of sweat
and what else skin deposits.
A tinge, dark as from seepage
not of sweat but of shadow,
lent character to varnish,
a personal brand, compiled
of manual residue.

The antique dealers call this
"patterns of wear." Probably
the rest of us would call it
something less grand, like "grunge."
No matter what we call it,
his mark is there to behold
long after the wear and tear
he lived with day after day
increased its hold upon him
until it left him for good.
I saw how it marked his life,
but still, for the life of me,
can't see in it a pattern—
meaning, a key to explain
just where it was things went wrong.

I need to keep looking, though,
unable to set it aside,
gripped by traces of his grip
and the darker marks unseen.

A BEACON

My father used to sit on summer evenings
on the terrace until well after dark fell,
smoking with his ashtray handy beside him
on a small redwood table that *his* father
had fashioned years back from his joiner's knowhow.
If you were outside, as I would be sometimes,
turning the hose off or padlocking the shed,
you could look toward the house and see him stationed,
or rather, just discern him draped in shadow,
making himself evident by inhaling,
rousing an ember-dot of hot vermilion,
as if his cigarette end took a cue from
fireflies glimmering in and above the grass,
but unlike them, finding no answering flash.

Somewhere I must still have his cigarette case,
a dressy thing he didn't for the most part
bother to use. I haven't used it either,
feeling it his, as shown by his initials.
Thinking about him sitting in the cooling,
deepening dark, I wish I had more often
sat down beside him so we could have traded
some comfortable words before the transient,
breathtaking bits of glow ended up in ash.

THE CUSTODY OF THE EYES

His mother always told him not to stare
at people of the kind that children stare at,
people she may have thought he'd take a scare at,
out on display, it could be, anywhere:

in stores, on sidewalks, lounging in the park,
missing an arm or leg that they were born with,
or more than one; or loudly trading scorn with
invisible enemies; or with eyes struck dark

staring themselves, sitting and selling matches.
He was a pliant child, and obeyed,
as wonder kindled (he was not afraid,
looking in only surreptitious snatches).

He wondered still, years on, why such protection
was furnished him. Or was it just another
lesson in better manners from his mother?
It didn't feel like that. It was projection,

he came at length to think, of her own fears
that all the rotten luck that life is host to
might possibly infect ones she was close to.
A shame she never learned over the years,

as her own share of damages amassed
to prey on her and those for whom she worried,
that it was wasted effort to have hurried
her child along as she marched blinkered past,

that eyes averted make no one immune
to ambushes like those she spent life fearing.
Pulled past by her, he couldn't keep from hearing
the match seller humming a happy tune.

THE WISH BONE

It was a huge one, harvested intact
from a Thanksgiving turkey and hung up
with some thought (wishful thinking) that it might
be coated gilt or glittery to make
a cunning trinket for the Christmas tree.
Somehow it missed the makeover. Come March,
still dangling from a cup hook in the pantry,
at last it caught their notice. What to do?
December wasn't due for a long time.
To make the best of it, they'd make a wish,
squared off against each other in the kitchen,
each gripping one of the upside-down
Y's angling limbs, each with a thumb
pressed against the stem right where it forked.
They'd play according to the children's rules
(as best they could remember that far back):
the longer breakaway, capped with the nexus,
would get the wish; saying the wish out loud
would mean it never, never would come true.
So they were silent, wishing they knew what.
Then: ready, set, yank! There was a snap,
sharp as when a stick tossed in a fire
explodes and spits out sparks; and something flew
briefly up, then plummeted: they each
were left holding a piece the same in length;
the third, a doubly amputated hub,
lay on the floor between them. Both said Oh!
and stepped back staring. Then they almost laughed,
but didn't, blindsided by stalemate,
their talismanic splinters telling merely
of bone gone brittle, wishes made too late.

CÉZANNE: "THE HOUSE WITH THE CRACKED WALLS"

Jutting up from the brow of the stony hill,
   presiding halfheartedly atop
a slope of green scrub and eroding boulders
   pumiced smooth like gravestones that the years
of derelict exposure have unlettered,
   this house lingers for now, evading
gravity's hunger that at a glance we know
   must have its way. Moldering yellow,
like some not-too-enticing slab of rat cheese,
   that wall is gouged with one off-center
erstwhile window, readier now to spill out
   darkness than let in daylight. Even
more unreassuring is the wanton crack,
   jabbing its cleavage from the faded
red-tiled roofline halfway down the languishing
   façade to where it stops like a jammed
zipper, holding in brittle check a hellbent
   cataract of yet more indwelling
darkness left by people who gave up and left.

   Why does it hurt so much to see it,
even without huffing uphill beneath that
   storm-intending sky? I never knew
the people who once lived there, never rested
   my hand on sun-warmed stucco, never
stepped around those corners into afternoon's
   east-facing shade. Yet I know the place
sufficiently to feel the wound it aches with,
   snared in its aura of destruction
just from viewing it shrunk and reproduced on

    a calendar page. A less extreme
dilapidation, I think, must be lurking
   beyond the margin as I stare at
this plight and descry, as though from the corner
   of an eye, my parents' failing porch,
sagging as time passed and incapacity,
   deepening, let it sag. That house was
white, not yellow. They moved from it years ago;
   now, side by side, they're done with moving.
And there is nothing now to be done about
   any of these things, unmendable,
except to turn the page as week follows week.

VESSEL

The imperturbability of objects:
consider, as to that, this christening bowl,
its sturdy pewter standing in for silver,
presented by my family in the mid-
nineteenth century to their creekside church—
wooden, plain, Ohio Presbyterian,
too plain, too small to need a greater font.

In 1897 that austere
edifice was torn from its foundation
when Wegee Creek, amok in a flash flood,
tumbled it downstream in several pieces.
Once the creek resumed its gravelly bed,
the bowl was found nested among some stones,
not even dented, only scratched a bit.
(Here, there seems to be a submerged theme
swirling about: sprinkling versus immersion.)
Rebuilding in a spot less near the water,
the church gave back the bowl to its presenters.
Clerical forebears on my mother's side,
first in Ohio, then in Pennsylvania,
used it to baptize the family's babies.
Perhaps it brought some luck to those occasions.

Even knowing its story, not much drama
seems to be disclosed in its design.
It has for ornament a single line
incised close to the rim, and for its base
a shallow-stepped pedestal that could rest
snugly in an officiating palm.
Grandfather, when he used it, would enhance

Philadelphia's tap water with a drop
or two of Jordan water from a bottle
some Presbyterian pilgrim had come home with.
Later, my mother kept it high and dry,
sometimes filling it with a spiky bunch
of desiccated blossoms of globe thistle—
a Scottish treatment. Since it's come to me,
I've kept it empty, leaving room for thoughts.

I can't look at the sheenless color of it
without being reminded of the lowering
mass of a thunderhead about to burst.
The unapologetic stern gray pewter,
mottled with age and lengthy lack of use
(no ministers of late for relatives),
looks able to withstand time's rudest inroads—
and why not? On its one foot it stood up
to water ramped in cataclysmic rage.
How soberly it wears its heritage.
Apotropaic, it outfaces storm.
Now, having been through a few storms myself,
I hold it as a token of continuance,
remembering as well that from it came,
five full decades after the flood's upheaval,
by water shed from my grandfather's fingers,
and by his saving words, my given name.

II
Now We Notice

BEFORE MY EYES

Crossing a fallow field on a hot
still day, I seem to be the only
body in motion, though a tiny
rickety sound tells me some insect
chafes away at a yearning solo,
so far unanswered. It's in the midst
of this noon-drowsy expanse that it
preempts my eye for a bare instant:
that uncanny emanation like
a sigh up from the blistering soil,
a formless flicker, not in itself
traceable, but in its displacement
of air at eye level suddenly
disclosing its presence close by like
a transparent cobra come upon
upreared and wavering in its dance.
Then gone, before I can even flinch.
It is as if I'd seen a tremor
but not the transient thing that trembled. …

I have come face to face with this
and its ilk before: I guess them now
to be some kind of a mini-thermal,
too low and listless to tower up
and make a tornado. Do they have
a name, or have they eluded that
by manifesting so fleetingly?
When I was a child, I didn't know
what to call them: no one could tell me.
Anything strange as that rates a name,
I thought, and still think. So I gave them

one that seemed to come out of nowhere
just as they did, fluttering into
verbalization in the heated
foraging on of my attention:
sun ghosts. Even now it seems right.

SUN SHOWER

    Shed literally out of the blue,
these drops make looking up irresistible,
    satisfying ourselves that yes, no
cloud is there on duty, measuring out now
    what it takes to dampen hikers' hair.
If the sun lit us from a lower angle,
    we might be walking through a rainbow
rather than just this briefly strewn display
    of shimmer that makes barely a dent
in the day's heavy air. Offbeat incidents
    like this exert a charm, no doubt by
being just as benign as unexpected,
    the spattering kept so slight, so bright
that shrill hints of cataclysm could
    be teased from it only by hidebound
Cassandras famished for new material.
    Let it go by, as we go by, as
a short walk in this or in any summer
    leaves nothing unerasably marked
in memory, as this surprise shower leaves
    no puddles, just drops the dirt swallows.
(There is, though, a modest lifting of spirits
    as the sun wicks off us the last traces.)
Folklore has made a joke of such rainfall:
    "The jackal's wedding"—so say the wits
in some parts of the world. In other places
    not well supplied with jackals, they need
a fallback phrase: "The devil's beating his wife."

DINOSAUR TRACKS

Beside the river where they used to wade
mornings or evenings in their hotter world,
relaxed as only those can be whose link
is soldered nicely high up on the food chain,
they've left a mincing trail of three-toed prints
in mud that time medusa'd into slabs
of sandstone brown as mud. The steps advance,
even less hurried now than when they first
pressed muck along their marshy avenue,
then vanish where the stratum is disrupted.

Each one about a man's handspan in size
and looking avian enough to plant
visions of carnivorous prototypes
of ostriches and emus (and in fact,
we're now informed such foragers wore feathers),
these tracks lead nowhere, and we're left to posit
the river of rivers in Connecticut
broadened and lush with swampy margins but
pursuing its primeval, silty creep
down reaches dense with hot fog and tree ferns,
as alien to us as any predator
traipsing along its banks. Again the world
is warming, sliding back toward a climate
like the one enjoyed by the old slashers,
and we, after scanning their once-soggy
plod into extinction, quicken our pace,
knowing what is forewarned and knowing too
we may at last leave less of an impression.

BELLIGERENTS

Back in the ragged woods
each crow has claimed a patch.
No changing neighborhoods
without a slanging match.

From where the pine trees tower
harsh voice and harsher voice
have jousted for an hour.
We've listened, not by choice.

Such wranglings, east or west,
are always the same story.
They need to guard the nest.
They've staked out territory.

Whose territory, though,
is what they can't agree on.
They want the world to know
they own a branch to be on,

that anyone who dares
to trespass should be wary.
This roosting place is *theirs*,
and no one else's aerie.

Just as the raucous folly
seemed bound to last till night,
it's met a check mid-volley.
Flyting gives way to flight.

The foiled conquistador
flaps somberly away;
the echoes promising gore
have nothing more to say.

The silence hovers, eerie,
until a smaller bird
peeps out a timid query
as though shy to be heard.

As featherless bystanders
we share his wonder: how
did two tough-lunged commanders
find courage to allow

their airing of aggression
room to de-escalate?
They settled for expression.
An enviable trait,

to bring an end to bluster
while it is still just noise.
If we in that passed muster
there would be fewer Troys.

"PITY THE MONSTERS!"

—Robert Lowell

Yes, at this late date, I pity them,
fang-flashers stuck with the dead-end job
of devouring bodies and / or souls
of victims hapless, foolhardy, or
corrupt, and always more on the way.
Think of Egypt's Eater of the Dead,
Ammit, equipped with crocodile head,
leopard torso, hippo hindquarters,
slumped and sulking beneath the balance
weighing the heart of each new would-be
tenant against the feather of truth.
Intent on nothing but the hoped-for
guilt overload that would fill her gorge,
she had to stay awake slavering
while Thoth droned out the court proceedings
and Anubis yawned, holding the scales.
Think of the Sphinx (the Grecian version),
part woman, part eagle, part lion,
roosting by the main road into Thebes,
a chimerical, bored toll-taker
programmed to plague each passerby
with her musty riddle, molting wings
unauthorized to flutter her off
her post even for calls of nature.
Think of chivalry-pestered dragons
who probably wanted nothing more
than a few well-spaced human gobbets
and peace and quiet while they caressed
their coin collections, snug in their caves.

Think of the centuries of bad press,
followed by years of no one taking
them seriously—to the point that
they became moth-eaten jabberwocks
scarcely able to alarm children.
It was their misfortune that we learned,
as soon as we did, not to fear them;
and after all, why should we ever
have done so, having earlier learned
to do unto others all the things
that made them infamous—things that now
we think may remain tolerable
if kept for the most part out of sight
while we dragoon the world purged of myth
into our own brittle regimen.

THE HOUSE OF THE TRAGIC POET

     would not seem all that tragic
except for our knowing it was blanketed
     in fuming pumice sixty feet thick,
first seared, then cooled in a petrifying bed.

     True, there are the painted walls
recycling the pathos of Troy's bitter tale.
     Bound for sacrifice, his daughter calls
to Agamemnon, whose ill-sworn vow would quail

     did he not hide his eyes, fend
away the sight of her sanctified slaughter.
     This household too lived blind to their end,
snug in their tasteful villa in this water-

     ing place of choice, adorning
the bay shore in view of the smoking mountain.
     Who can know what the morrow may bring,
was their art's frescoed message, and the fountain

     of blitzing ash drove it home,
obliterating their resort town idyll
     and splintering morale back in Rome.
Precious few outran the fiery overkill;

     if some from this sedate
family did, another scene they'd lived with
     might later have made them contemplate:
Helen boarding ship, embarking on her myth

    unforewarned she would return
to a dull mate's duller realm, there to remain
    a wan trophy, having seen Troy burn
to a black mound, seen her lover's army slain.

    Was she prepared to survive
the overthrow of her adopted city?
    Or did she feel, shocked to be alive,
something that scorched beyond all fear and pity?

LACHRYMATORY

Fashioned in teardrop style,
this Greek or Roman vial,

doll-sized and opaline,
like others of its line

is famed for having kept
the tears that mourners wept

processing toward the grave
of each they could not save.

They sealed their trace of salt
with loved ones in the vault.

The tribute of their tears
was meant to outlast years;

the years were meant to pass
and leave intact the glass

that held encased what grief
extorts for its relief.

The cloudy little flask
accomplished half the task,

won for its unmarred self
space on an esthete's shelf,

but let the tears take flight
sometime in the long night

before the fastened tomb
opened to air its gloom.

Now, what is here to see
is sheer metonymy—

container for contained.
If those old tears remained,

would that add emphasis?
Perhaps. But I think this

vessel enshrining void
conveys what time destroyed

far more than tears once shed
could mollify the dead.

The vacancy men face
in every time and place

it can and will express—
this dram of emptiness.

ON THE DEATH OF WILMER MILLS

This bruise discoloring my upper arm
came, as most of them do, quite by surprise,
bumping into a post or someone's elbow.
The run-in shows itself beneath the skin,
the busy lymph collected in a pond
of beige and gray, paling to feathered edges.
It pays witness to the world's buffetings,
and at a touch recalls its birth in pain.

Just so with this imponderable event.
Decades too soon, disheartening to grasp,
your death has put its mark upon the mind,
a thought that lingers, waking to itself
with each recurrent impact of your absence,
a pain unfinished now that yours is finished.

A CONFIRMATION

The shadow of a falling leaf
plummeted down the page I read,
as if enlisted for a brief
enactment of what there was said

sadly of dying generations
ceding their glory to the ground.
Foliage, flesh, the pride of nations
pledged to one end. I turned around

too late to see it join the crowd,
the yellow ruck fast thickening.
The lawn was chilled below its shroud.
The pace of loss was quickening.

Of course the stricken world outside
had been destruction-bound for days.
Should words that held me occupied
have better mirrored each grim phase?

Perhaps. I only know it took
that shadow of one casualty
dropping through margins of the book
to bring home fall in full to me.

SEPTEMBER TOADSTOOLS

Fall is their springtime. As the flowers fade
and foresight nudges squirrels to plump their hauls,
and leaves let go, skeletonizing shade,
these flourish, lifting spongy parasols.

Now days turn duller; more and more emerge
out of the dingy trapdoors of the soil,
muscling up along the lawn's damp verge,
burgeoning while the fruits of summer spoil.

Hobnobbing now in squads, in fairy rings,
in straggling queues, lopsided pentacles,
they party on through all the perishings
that set the stage for their conventicles.

A limbless neck, brown gills, and bulbous pate
is no one's notion of a neat profile.
Poisonous, too, most likely. They would rate
low as to virtue, as they do for style.

Give them some points, though, for vitality.
Fed on decay, they get their spores around—
one fresh start, anyway, in this locality
where so much else is dying to the ground.

WINTER STARS

Orion's back. The same old sight:
holding aloft his lion's pelt,
the hunter strides across the night.
His sword, his club, his glittering belt

denote that now, as every year,
that greater belt, the zodiac,
makes room for him and all his gear.
He knows his job—to stay on track

hunting he knows what on the loose
so many light years from the ground.
His shoulder's red with Betelgeuse.
His prey, once more, will go unfound.

Brawnily awesome, not too wise,
he finds the longer nights call forth
in him a lust to roam our skies.
When winds pour fury from the north,

most of the rest of us agree
to stay indoors and let them howl,
enwrapped in comfort such as he
would scorn as he conducts his prowl.

Now in a night approaching zero,
eyeing the sparklers in his belt,
we'll let him—why not?—play the hero.
When he moves on, the ice will melt.

HANGING ON

Still greening that old lady's door,
the Christmas wreath, when March came round,
was not such out-of-phase décor
as long as snow festooned the ground.

But now the April rains have streaked
the crimson bow a mottled puce.
Needles and all have been antiqued;
exiting winter less than spruce,

it casts more gloom than merriment.
Doesn't she realize, peering out,
the world is halfway into Lent?
Birds are back, cherries about

to blossom, but at her address
it's still Noel. Now passing by,
I think of her at little less
than ninety-five and once more try

to grasp how that must be, and fail.
She teeters out on canes each day
like clockwork to pick up her mail.
Maybe she's let her trappings stay

to show that hurry's out of place,
to stem the rush of feast and fast.
Slowing to something like her pace
I wonder how long this can last.

AN ARRANGEMENT OF DRIED FLOWERS

What was it that our friend said?
"Bad feng shui."
They're off-putting, looking dead
but not all the way.

Odors among which waded
honeybees
are gone from these odd-shaded
arid effigies.

The yellows brought to a halt
short of rust,
the whites brittle as rock salt,
hardened pinks—all must

cast more of a charm on some
audience
that does not regard as glum
would-be permanence.

Give suchlike to the long-range
astronaut,
cabined light years, seeking change
from what flesh has wrought;

or to kings tucked in stone sar-
cophagi,
whose fine linens daubed with tar
keep their tissues dry.

For us, though, these arrested
blooms inspire
an old thought: time, unbested,
wants each sprig drier.

And who cares to recall that
steady leak
draining softness, scent, all that
even as we speak? …

NOW WE NOTICE

The rug has faded from the sun's
daily high tides: a background once
as red as blood is brickdust now.
The arabesques of indigo
have traded in their midnight look
for gauzy twilight. All this took
how long? Who wants to count the years?
And even if the rug had ears,
can we reproach it for the way
it let some color ebb each day?
It didn't have a choice: it lay there.
Choosing for now to let it stay there,
we take a dimmer view of light
that rushes colors into sight
in a bright instant, only to
reclaim them as its rightful due
by dribs and drabs, by daily stints
contriving these depleted tints.
More than the sun must be behind
what's happened. Guess the mastermind.
What's left is dignified and wan,
a stoic weft to ponder on,
whose paling pattern represents
the least of time's embezzlements.

III

A Late Spring, and After

THE TALLY

Mother first, now my wife.
Dead within a year.
A joke unfunny life
has foisted on me here.

Past sixty, orphanhood
can't be unexpected.
It came; I understood.
Grief was calm, collected.

But that just months ahead
there would be a second
farewell to be said—
that I had not reckoned.

One, two: each blow hit home.
Each left the house more quiet.
Each time, the patient loam
obtained some profit by it.

The orchestra has stopped.
But faintly, unabating
though the baton has dropped,
two notes go on vibrating.

One, two: insistent pair
clinging to every thought.
Murmured to vacant air,
"One, two" adds up to nought.

One, two: the digits can't
supply those fingers' touch
now no more extant,
neither caress nor clutch.

One, two: my footsteps roam
from empty street to street.
Some tireless metronome
sets the relentless beat.

One, two: the pace I keep
requires no grace of art.
Whether I wake or sleep,
despoiled again, my heart

does all it knows to do:
as if it overheard,
it keeps the count—one, two—
will, till I make a third.

WHAT HAPPENED

When the doctor told me that nothing more could be done beyond "making her comfortable," I asked them to bring her home. I was unready, but the house was made ready. She would have to be in the living room, it had the most floor space. We pushed back the sofas, took out the coffee table, rolled up the rug. The Hospice man wheeled in the surprisingly portable hospital bed and set it up in the center of the room, demonstrated all its robotic tilting tricks. Then two gigantic ambulance men brought her up the front steps and in. The nurse soon had her settled.

*

Our son Tony and I took instructions about the oxygen, about the morphine (at first, a dropperful every two hours, then doses closer together as things went downhill at an even faster rate). I grew proficient quickly with the dropper, trying not to think too much about how this now was all that I could do for her. The Hospice promised as much morphine as she needed, which turned out to be just two days' worth.

*

But there was one thing at least still to be done besides giving morphine. The Rector came on the first afternoon and anointed her. We stood by and fumbled through the words, and I felt that something fitting was being accomplished. I watched as the spot on her forehead that I used to kiss received the sign of the Cross.

*

She seemed to know she was home but didn't speak, seemed to be awake but not awake. I had been worried the cats might try to jump up, but they stayed clear, unnerved perhaps by the bed's mechanism, or by the change in her. I kept up a one-sided conversation. They said that hearing was the last thing to go.

*

I had just stepped out of the room when Tony called me back: "You better come." She had stopped breathing. Air nestled obligingly about her face but would not be drawn. She looked to be at peace, if lack of expression means peace has been achieved. Every plane and angle of her frail face, motionless on the pillow, imprinted itself unsparingly on my mind. Her gray-green eyes, which always reminded me of the sea-washed pebbles she liked to collect, had turned to a flatter gray. On her left ring finger were the wedding ring I had given her forty-five years ago and the engagement ring from a few years later (it took a while to afford a ring with a stone). The Hospice nurse removed them and gave them to me, and folded her hands the way they do with dead people in the movies. The undertaker arrived. Tony took me out in the backyard until we heard his van going down the driveway.

*

The remaining stock of morphine could not legally be passed on to another patient. The nurse disposed of it deftly, pouring the vials into a small pile of cat litter, which then was bagged and thrown out. As I watched, I thought crazily: "So no one can get high / On what helped her to die." I called our daughter Catherine in Charleston and began making arrangements.

*

I know, each asterisk seems to say, "And then?" It astonished me that things could just go on happening, to me and around me, after what had happened, could go on as if nothing had happened, as if there were still some point in going on, after my best reason for being was gone out of reach.

*

The same man came back the next day to reclaim the bed. After he wheeled it out, and also collected the oxygen tank and the other things—all this in a matter of fifteen minutes—I stood and looked at the bare stretch of floor, and wondered if it would ever sound right to me, after this, to call it the living room.

A LATE SPRING

She died on Mother's Day.
Our son stood close to me.
What more is there to say?

Spring had just come to stay,
too late for her to see.
She died on Mother's Day,

next to the thin bouquet
he'd gathered hastily.
What more is there to say?

Cold hung on, had its way
down to the last degree.
She died on Mother's Day,

those few flowers on her tray,
buds lagging on each tree.
What more is there to say

now, when the warming clay
seems pleased to let life be?
She died on Mother's Day.
What more is there to say?

THE LOSS OF THE JOY OF COOKING

The book is missing. Somewhere in the house,
misshelved, or at the bottom of some pile,
its columned pages keep their measurements,
ingredients, oven times, and helpful hints
beyond perusal in a fat, useless wad.

The island kitchen counter lets me have
my pick of sides to feel myself marooned on.
I push ahead without a recipe,
halving quantities of what I have
somehow to make edible without
the stir of appetite.

                    We used to work
together at it, each on a different side,
she stirring, measuring, tasting, I
chopping, dicing, mincing as required.
Rocking the blade the way she showed me to,
I freed from each raw thing a smell we liked:
the garlic's earthy reek, the ginger's sting,
the anise wisping up from celery leaves.

Now I look at the counter's empty side
and listen to the onion I hacked up
sputtering angrily, intense but futile,
faltering as its fund of hoarded tears
dissolves in the hot oil that some hunks
of meat will sear in next. It probably
isn't quite right (like so much else these days)
but it will do: I need to make it do.

The book is missing. Even if it's found
and followed to the letter, there will still
be loss, the unlisted ingredient,
throwing the best efforts out of balance.
It bakes itself into what's left of life.
The cold plate waits. Nothing now tastes the same.

VOICE MAIL

Well-meaning, tactless, spooked, or simply clueless,
callers wonder why it is still *her* voice
they hear if I'm not there to pick up the phone,
politely asking them to leave a message.
I wish I had an answer, but I haven't.
Am I an archivist, that I should keep
her few seconds of gatekeeping as if
they were historic, like those nip-and-tuck
rescued cylinders from which Tennyson
goes on declaiming, an embattled grandee
sunk deep in time, ravaged by all its static?
(She sounds better than that, if more perfunctory.)
How would she feel? Impatient with my failure
to bring things up to date? People who call
are put off by my failure to "move on."

Once or twice, knowing how crazy it was,
I've dialed my own number just to hear her,
stopping myself short from leaving a message.
I couldn't ask her—could I?—to call me back.
I think the utterly disquieting truth
is that holding her calm voice to my ear
even now feels to me like protection,
and that I fear erasing it would set
a seal for all time on the house's silence,
unbroken now unless I talk to myself.

YOUR HAND

In a house filled with paper I can't go long
without turning up a leaf you'd written on—
an address, a recipe, a list of Things
To Do, many of which escaped getting done,
and now in many cases won't be needed.
I read each scrap as if it were a letter,
realizing how rarely we wrote each other
anything more than refrigerator notes,
living together almost forty-five years.
Even on some old grocery list, creased-up
and come upon in a spring jacket pocket
your hand is firm, incisive, calligraphic,
stroke by stroke set down with an unassuming
elegance. No need for a graphologist
to tell me how true to yourself your writing
was, and remains. I used to enjoy watching
your hand leading the pen in a quick line-dance,
cursive trimly attentive no matter what
trivial matter made you pick up a pen.

Deft characters that inscribed your character.
I wish now I had told you your handwriting
was beautiful, the way I told you sometimes
(not often enough) how beautiful I thought
your hands, both of them, were in every gesture.
I look at oddments of paper and I think:
Your handwriting. Your hand, writing. Your hand.
I think of how my own hand, writing this now,
held your pale hand until it no longer felt
familiar, seized from mine by a colder grip.

CLOCKWORK SONNET

For months on end the clock you gave to me
has sat unwound, deprived of tick and chime.
Somehow I've managed to mislay the key.
My mind sways in a stalemate over time:
Hours, when they were ours, were not hours,
they were unfenced green fields to wander through.
Hours, when they were ours, were not ours
to keep. How can these trite things both be true?

Someday, it may be, if the key is found
I'll do as you would, crank the idle hands
tight for their tut-tut through the daily round.
And we? Will our hands meet when time unhands
me in my turn? Those who claim yes or no
must know something I don't. But time will show.

THE SUN ROOM PLANTS

I water them, and watch as their green lives
give up the ghost for all that I can do.
Without her care it seems that nothing thrives.
They grope for light they lost when she withdrew.

Each root and leaf and intervening stem
weakens without her gift for nurturing.
Could I repot them?   —But to look at them
hurts, and confirms they never were my thing.

To them it hadn't mattered much what season
was in control of things beyond the glass.
Their cherished status offered them a reason
to dream their summer had no need to pass.

Dreams cheat me too. Forty-four summers take
leave of me now each morning when I wake.

FLUID OUNCES

Rummaging in a drawer, my fingers felt
something cool and smooth and round—no, ovoid—
which, not too surprisingly, turned out
to be a bottle of her latest perfume.
Heavy for its size, clear glass half full
of a clear liquid. I could look through it
and see the room rendered a bit off-kilter.
I hesitated. Then I opened it.

It smelled like spring, or like spring ought to smell:
light and ferny, lively but elusive.
I thought of her neatly painting on a drop
or two in the soft hollow behind an earlobe,
feeling the cool fragrance meeting her warmth.
I thought of her hand placing the flask where mine
had bumped into it so many months later.

I know where it is now. I can revisit it,
and have, helplessly drawn to this metonymy
two-timing me each time I pick up the scent.
As if a bottle unstoppered were a life
restarted, for a few moments (seconds, really)
it fills the room with figments of her nearness.
Then it fades, lost in a brooding pall
of vacancy that stings the eyes and nostrils
like smoke left over after a house burns down.

THROUGH A GLASS, DARKLY

For someone who didn't make much use of mirrors,
she picked up quite a few of them over the years,
animating bare spaces with mimicking glass.
Each time a new one appeared I would ask, while she
hammered a hook in, "Do we really need that there?"
And she would say, "Look how it makes the room bigger,"
or give as a good reason, "It doubles the light."
She didn't linger in front of any of them.
Even before the grand one above her dresser
she would pause only briefly, tightening earrings,
smoothing a fold, or checking the length of a scarf.
I gave a lot of her scarves to the Hospice Shop.

Grubby with dust I keep forgetting to wipe off,
the dormant glass accepts neglect patiently till
I make the mistake of standing in front of it.
Then I see that her ideas on mirrors, while true,
don't tell the whole story: this one of hers, in what
I still call our bedroom, does make the room bigger,
but does it by making emptiness more pronounced;
it doubles the light, but doubles the darkness too.
And if I look at myself standing in her place
I soon grow sick of my material being,
my helpless casting of shadows, my sham of a
life persisting, my habit of taking up space.

AFTERTHOUGHT

She, above all, enlarged my life and brightened it.
Even now, if I look in memory's mirror
there is some peace to be had when the mind's daylight
defies chronology, finding us side by side,
or cleaving together in the solemnity
of our bodies' worship, and by some great mercy
forgetful of all but time's best gifts and heedless
of any moment beyond the one we were in.

EIGHT MONTHS LATER

A morning early in winter: half asleep,
I lay as I had too often done before,
gulled into thinking life was back to normal.
Then I opened my eyes and when I saw
the bed empty beside me, I knew it wasn't.

I got up even though it was too early.
Sitting down to cold cereal, unrested,
I looked out to see dawn twilight paling.
And it was only by the purest chance
my eyes were raised so as to see the deer,
a young male with a respectable rack
of antlers, crossing over the cleared hill,
pacing out of the woods on the other side,
neither dawdling nor in a great hurry,
merging soon with the stand of trees he aimed for.

I thought of how she would have liked to see this.
We used to watch them together, talking in murmurs,
moved by how much at home they were in the world.
I hadn't seen any lately, grouped or single.
I was just about to push back my chair
when his mate appeared out of the same covert
and walked the path he had pioneered on hard
frostbitten turf, till she too blurred out of view.
Voiceless, he must have stamped, the way they do,
to let her know that it was safe to follow.
With the same measured pace, undeviating,
she had moved as though magnetized to join him.

So: was this an emblem served up with breakfast?
It had some weak points as an analogy,
since in our case she was the first to set out,
while I seem to be waiting for directions.
What I derived from that impassive treeline
was the thought of them out of sight together,
after their crossing of that cold, barren place,
as surely, as invisibly together
as they had been, as they meant always to be.

ENVOY

How can I save my words from growing faint
In their attempt to summon back the same
Long sunlit hours that once were yours and mine?
All cast in shadow now? Not if complaint
Rewords itself to praise. Graced with your name,
Your musing glow, light quickens every line.

IV

Ferrying

BY THE POND

Dragonflies dart, basking turtles doze.
      Noon is furnishing
   water with a trance that grows
   deep from daily burnishing.

Passersby who automatically
      give slime a bad name
   should slow down, see what I see.
   It might nudge them to reframe

received opinions. At the pond's edge
      turbid sepia
   sprawls unlovely from the sedge
   to meet what seems to be a

fabulous floating green mantilla—
      spun of such a shade
   as if one might distill a
   thready essence out of jade

or other swag equally precious,
      then wide-cast a net
   of it, close-woven, lustrous,
   each intense diatom set

gemlike, snug among gemlike fellows.
      The Great Smaragdine
   Tablet (raft-borne, I suppose)
   might fling out a sheen as fine,

    vibrant with the workings of the sun
          that keeps giving hints
      of fire fused in every one
      of these algae pooling glints.

Yes, if you insist: a trick of light.
        But so too are all
    favors caught and prized by sight
    that prodigal sun lets fall.

THREE RIDDLES FROM THE EXETER BOOK

Riddle 27

From groves and green hills girdling the city,
from dales and downs, holding me dear,
foragers fan out far to fetch me.
Once wafted on wings through warm bright air,
I was put under thatch by practiced porters.
In time attendants gave me a tub-bath.
Now I bind men and belabor them brutally;
any young tough guy I'll toss on his tail
as quick as I can some old curmudgeon.
Any galoot going at me to grapple,
setting his strength against my strength,
soon realizes he's ripe for a rest,
finds himself flat on his foolish back
if he dares to endure what I dish out.
Gone all gimpy, gassing off big-time,
strength siphoned off, his sodden brain,
dazed feet and hands don't heed his edicts.
Tell what I'm called, daily taking captive
tyros whose trouncing ought to teach them,
but after each bout just beg for more.

Riddle 35

Dank earth, dealing dumbfounding chill,
first brought me forth, fostered my breaking
clear of its clutching inner keep.
My musing mind mulls over my nature:
wrought not of wool of ram or wether
nor of the hairs of wild beasts hunted
and closely woven with wondrous craft.
No woof, no warp, no weaving made me.
No taut thread hummed as I took form,
no shuttle sang me its rasping song,
no treadle thumped, keeping time with the tune.
Those exquisitely embroidering worms
whose caches of yellow silk crowd cocoons,
who spin their skeins with the skill of Fates,
forbore to fashion me of their fabric.
Even so, to every end of the earth,
with worthy experts offering witness,
people proclaim me the kind of apparel
a man can count on in a tight corner.
Might and mettle meet in my mesh.

You, whose wit can winnow this welter,
culling out clues, now use your cunning
to reach the answer this riddle requires:
lay out language to label this garment.

Riddle 70, lines 5-6

High on this headland day and night I stand
and show a blushing cheek, but feel no shame.
Men out cruising ogle me, weigh my worth.
Hear my solicitation: what's my name?

PATHS CROSSING

Careering composedly over the road before us,
with a purposeful lope and pennant of rust-red tail,
accustomed to getting there fast, without any fuss
(*there* being now a weed patch abutting the county jail),

the fox, having come at a bound out of nowhere, regained
his invisibility thanks to the snarl of scrub
that so imperturbably took him in headlong. We strained
our eyes in vain for an encore, then gave them a rub

of wonderment as you might after seeing the streak
of a meteor darting through space: while not celestial,
this dash of his featured a gravity-taunting technique
that shaped a series of springs into something less bestial

than balletic. There wasn't a chance to applaud him, though—
he'd raced off into his otherness, and we had places to go.

NEWS ITEM

Five thousand red-winged blackbirds,
oddly aloft at night,
got flight directions backwards
in this, their final flight.

Even as they were winging
their way across the sky
some force possessed them, flinging
them down to earth, to die.

On New Year's Eve they bought it.
And the macabre scene
was such that people thought it
prefigured Halloween.

A kamikaze action?
A bow to Newton's Law?
Still, no great satisfaction
to folks in Arkansas.

The town of Beebe starred in
the news—no more ignored,
with every lawn and garden
hosting the fallen horde.

Their mourner: one sad phoebe.
No lowering of flags.
The citizens of Beebe
got out their garbage bags.

Far more than four-and-twenty,
and none alive to sing,
they left us groundlings plenty
of cause for pondering.

If we were ancient, Roman,
and worried over Fate,
we might call this an omen.
We might haruspicate.

We won't. But still, we wonder,
made restless in our beds
by the night skies we're under,
by what's above our heads.

SHARED HABITAT

In this closet-cave
hang three black collapsible
companions at rest

between outings. No
mosquitoes here to feast on,
and when they unfurl

it's always raining—
no bugs outside then, either.
What do they live on?

Are we starving them?
Could that be why they manage
to detach themselves

so often from us?
Periodic escapes don't
make them better off.

And in fact, nestled
in entryway somnolence,
they seem unperturbed;

unlike some species
they send no yips or twitters
across the twilight.

Are they content, then,
with letting storms bounce off their
popped-up repellence,

or just smug, thinking
they know what clouds are brewing
better than we do?

Hugging their hinged ribs,
perhaps they chuckle, when we're
well out of earshot:

"Mad torrents! Savage
winds ramping up to blow this
setup inside out!"

Well: could they be right?
Rain's starting. But I'll bet this
house will last the night.

LAPCAT

Although I don't have all that large a lap,
when I sit down within her observation
Pandora hops up with the combination
purr and meow that means she wants a nap.

Curling herself into a doughnut pose,
nestling nose on tail, some edges of her
hang off; she doesn't mind. Meanwhile, above her,
the book I'm reading, packed with leaden prose,

could brain her if it slithered from my grip.
She trusts me (why?) not to disturb her slumber.
There have been times, too many now to number,
when a cramped need to shift a leg or hip

led me to fidget, her to twitch an ear
or part her lids to signal disapproval.
Unrest prolonged goads her to self-removal,
but grudgingly, and soon enough she's here

and hopping up again. Upholstery,
carpets or cushions, all are uncompelling,
even her padded basket. Some indwelling
magnetic force zeroes her in on me.

Clearly she's got me where she wants me, serving
as her obliging mattress, if you will.
I've grown resigned to it by now, but still,
to know she owns me is a bit unnerving.

I picture us transposed, but still a pair:
I in a luxury of unconcern
settled down on her, she with much to learn
plodding through footnotes, pinned down in our chair.

What are the odds she'd make that genus-leap?
Humanity's no fate she'd bow to tamely.
In her good time she'll wake and trot off gamely.
I notice now my foot has gone to sleep.

SENSITIVE PLANT

(Mimosa pudica)

Though it may look as self-possessed
as any plant safe in a pot,
this one is different from the rest.
Most of them trust me. This does not.

Its feathery leaf, a leaf all fringe,
will at my inadvertent touch
collapse into a total cringe,
fold up to hug itself in such

a visceral flinch I jerk away
myself, outmastered in surprise.
How it mimes *Noli me tangere*
with muscles none to galvanize

is for a botanist to explore.
(It should be hardier, you'd think,
transplanted from a forest floor.)
But I, abashed to see it shrink,

begin to think of other creatures,
sentient or not, unequally
equipped with such defensive features.
How many have been jarred by me,

meandering past, with inattention
blurring the bounds in which I live?
More victims than I care to mention.
Which of us now is sensitive?

NEW YEAR'S WISH

Raised and splayed like a traffic signal—STOP—
a small red mitten caps a fence spike, perching
hopefully before a city backdrop
of snow heaps and gray stone. The owner's searching
his pockets somewhere, coming up empty-handed,
cold, and wondering what will Mother say.
("The second in three days!") Pathetic, stranded,
up against winter ranged for a long stay,
will it be rescued? Walking by, we slip
into a warm red woolen wishful spell:
Let losses halt. Let the glum, icy grip
that hobbles life give way; let days go well
for those who work and worry, watch and wait.
And let each errant mitten find its mate.

HER MOTHER'S SEASHELL

sat on the bedside table, almost
as big as the black phone next to it.
Each week she could count on being called
to talk long distance to grandparents
and didn't need to be told, when at
loose ends, to pick up the shell and press
her ear close to it, as to a more
primitive receiver, listening
to what was said to be the ocean
going on about its restless business.
(That was long distance, too: the nearest
beach was two states away.) The sea voice
was neither daunting nor alluring,
just white noise emitted like a drift
of air escaping an unmapped cave.
Always there for her, the sound announced
itself in that marine dial tone,
more an inarticulate prelude
than a message delivering sense.
In any case, the shell, to look at,
did not strike her as being like
a mouth itching to chat. The smooth pink sheen
devolving back into its hidden
labyrinth was more convincingly
an ear waiting for her to whisper
back to it something private, a secret.
She never did, though, having a child's
too keen sense of what would be silly.
It was years later she thought of this
and wondered what she could have told it,
couched in terms it might be in tune with—

Sometimes I feel flung up by the tide
or *Sometimes I feel empty inside?*
Too late now, though, to experiment.
The shell was gone, shattered by someone's
slapdash dusting. It would have listened
in calm, mother-of-pearl inertia,
yielding back its never-ending sigh.

AN EARLY SKIRMISH

"Leave me alone!" the boy shouts,
scuffling free of his sister's
reach, monkeying to the top
of the monkey bars, and there
roosting in precarious
isolation, sending down
defiant looks, trading taunts,
and finally just sitting
sullenly, an eight-year-old
Simeon Stylites. (They've
been wrangling all morning long,
making the playground vibrate
with sequential eruptions
of sibling rivalry.) When
she and her friends decide to
go somewhere (anywhere
less boring and less hot) and
skip off, his sense of drama
keeps him grimly pedestaled
on into lunchtime. At length
he tarzans down and stomps home,
past the one sun-blistered bench
occupied as always by
that weird old retiree, a
threadbare local oracle
who could (but won't) tell him what
he hasn't got a clue of:
what it's like—no, what it is—
to be left alone for real.

TRANSFORMATION SCENE

The days go slowly but the years go fast.
Old movies used to bridge the story's gaps
by morphing falling leaves to frantic snow,
or showing pages of a massive book
madly flipping themselves, or, desperately,
superimposing on the hapless background
an hourglass turning cartwheels. When the cast
came back after such intervals, their costumes
were updated, their erstwhile raven tresses
were streaked with white, or thinned, or salt-and-peppered.
It was crude, but what else could they do,
collapsing decades into ninety minutes?
The dents and scuffs that time supposedly
had put upon those celluloid personae
were in the end no harder to believe
than what the forward tug of time had done
to maim or to refine their inner selves,
as the remaining reel was left to show.

You think of this when the old friend turns up
after how many years you can't remember,
and each of you feels awkwardly confronted,
making what you hope is not too blatant
an inventory of the other's features
that do or don't fit the remembered image.
Any dissimulation, though, is wasted;
you're both as obvious in your intent
as cats competing in a staring match.
Once recognition stifles disbelief,
it seems you each still have a part to play.
You're on! By now it's too late to be asking
where and when you might have come by a script.

FERRYING

We took that ferry ride too many times.
It was a way to shave an hour off
the trip, less of a grind than the Expressway.
But it was boring, and the only way
to put up with it was to ritualize it.
So, with the car stowed in what I guess
would not, on ferry boats, be called the hold,
we stood on deck and watched the concrete pier
receding, watched where we had been get small.
We felt the engine's hum more than we heard it.
Something kept us determined to look back
until land disappeared, and this at last
was like an upper and a lower lid,
sky and water, gradually colluding
until the rickety, unlovely port
was gone as if our own eyes closed on it.
Then for a short time there was only water
lapping away on all sides, nothing yet
apparent as a haven in the offing—
so we noticed, turning about face. Somehow
we never felt as drawn to that so-far-
unspotted destination as we'd been
to what we had seen vanish. At midpoint,
the ferry's twin passed by us with a hoot,
chugging to where we'd come from, as if both
boats were hauled along by a double pulley.

Car fumes, boat fumes, just a slim whiff of salt;
blasé occasional seagulls, more than occasional
children bickering, parents buying them soda.
We must have felt at least a dim unease

at the hiatus that our fare had paid for;
we kept close to each other the whole time.
The water now was army-colored, empty
except for the odd sailboat in the distance,
and except for our own cargo of noise
the Sound was largely silent.

                        It's been years
since I have driven on or off that boat.
Now when it swashes into my dreams, it's all
much as it was on the vibrating deck
except that I'm alone and facing forward,
for a change having become impatient
to see what hasn't yet come into view.
All around me wrinkles that sullen water
we got across so often in one piece,
even emptier now than I remember.
I always wake before shore is in sight.

WINTER SUNSET

Veiled by a winter scrim
of early evening haze,
the sun gives but a dim
impression of its blaze,

barren of rays, a disc
of crimson trundling west,
peered after without risk
by eyes not seared but blessed

by what pours without stint
on ground clenched tight with cold:
rose, purple, pink, each tint
touched at its edge with gold.

Could there be more to see?
Replacing each bold swatch
comes twilight's clarity.
It is for that I watch:

when, in a moment's trance,
viewer and viewed are one.
Earth itself seems to glance
back after day just done.

The year '15 retires.
In '16 so will I.
Surveying these banked fires
beneath a darkening sky,

I'd say this landscape frames
hints of how best to go.
Others may crash in flames.
My goal is afterglow.

NOTES

"The House of the Tragic Poet": This building, one of the villas of Pompeii buried by the eruption of Vesuvius in 79 CE, was so named by modern archeologists because of its numerous frescoes depicting scenes from Greek mythology, and mosaics, one of which depicts actors preparing for a performance. The house was excavated in 1824.

A Late Spring, and After: My wife died on May 11, 2014. The poems in this section were written between January and August, 2015.

"By the Pond": The Great Smaragdine Tablet, also called the Emerald Tablet, is a brief Hermetic text whose earliest (sixth to eighth centuries) source is in Arabic. It was translated into Latin in the twelfth century and was thereafter intently studied by alchemists, including Isaac Newton, who made his own English translation of it. It speaks forcefully and cryptically of the unity of all things and propounds the doctrine of correspondences: in Newton's rendering, "that which is below is like that which is above & that which is above is like that which is below to do the miracles of one only thing." W. B. Yeats alludes to the Tablet and especially to this assertion in the second of his "Supernatural Songs." In my own poem, the phrase "the workings of the sun" echoes part of the Tablet's final sentence.

"Three Riddles from the Exeter Book": A tenth-century codex, the Exeter Book is the largest known collection of Old English literature. None of the ninety-odd riddles in the text are accompanied by answers; modern translations usually supply answers based on scholarly consensus. In the case of these three riddles, the suggested answers are: 27, mead; 35, a coat of mail; 70, ll. 5-6, a lighthouse. My renderings are influenced by the original verse forms, but allow themselves numerous liberties.